YELL GOD AND LIVE!

CARL MCROY

Printed by
College Press
Collegedale, TN 37315
www.cplitho.com

To my wife, Luceta:

Thanks for being my paraclete when I felt like giving up on this project. I pray these words will help comfort you as you reflect on the recent loss of your Giant.

CONTENTS

1

WHY?

Why does life hurt so much? Why is life so unfair? Why do bad things happen to good people? Why do good things happen to bad people? Why does a chain-smoker live to be eighty while an eight-year-old dies of cancer? Why do drunk drivers walk away unscathed after sending others to their graves? Why do babies die in the womb?

Why do tornados suck people out of their hiding places but leave china cabinets untouched? Why do the rich get richer while the poor get poorer? Why do banks get bailed out while homeowners get thrown out? Why do people go on shooting rampages in elementary schools? Why can't the police do something? Why can't the doctors do something? Why doesn't the president do something? Why doesn't God do something?

Why didn't God answer my prayer? Why didn't God perform a miracle the way He did in the Bible? Why do church folk censor my questions? Why do I feel so alone with so many people around? Why doesn't anyone understand me? Why was I born this way? Why was I born at all? Why keep going through the motions? Why not just give up? Why? Why? WHY?

One-word wrecking ball

One of the first and most persistent questions in life is, "Why?" It is arguably the shortest sentence in the English language. Yet "Why?" is a wrecking ball to the sophisticated intellect. A three-year-old armed with this one-word inquiry can confound philosophers about whether realism or relativism is the best perspective for a post-positivist world. Although the three-year-old can't even pronounce, let alone understand, any philosophical jargon, his monosyllabic interrogation will confound the wisdom of the sages. *Ahem, translation please.* Just talk to a curious toddler and you'll quickly see that you don't know as much as you thought you knew!

As we age, we may settle for the way things are without asking why until a crisis comes. Then our "why reflex" is revived, and we add to the list above.

Many religious people say it's blasphemy to ask why. Usually it's people who don't have good answers who get annoyed with the questions. "How dare you question God?"

I respond to the "saint" who asks this question with "Is your God so insecure that He can't be questioned?" How can the "why" question, the most childlike of verbal reflexes, be so offensive to God? What happened to the longsuffering, sympathetic, omniscient, omnipotent deity that we've been told about? If such inquiries arouse God's indignation, does that mean He's insecure or that His well of wisdom has run dry?

Lukewarm backwash

God is still the source of the wells springing up out of the hearts of every true disciple of Christ. "Whoever drinks the water I give them will never thirst. Indeed, the water I give them will become in them a spring of water welling up to eternal life" (John 4:14).

Unfortunately, His *mis*-representatives sometimes make it difficult to distinguish their babbling brooks from the wells of living water. But don't stop searching because you've been offered lukewarm backwash from broken cisterns. God gave us His word so we can know the pure from the polluted.

Many who thought they were simply opening another ordinary book discovered that the Bible supplies streams of hope in the desert of despair. Explore the sacred pages for yourself, and you'll see that much of what you've heard about God didn't come from Him.

Many of the religious prohibitions that impede open communion with God are based more on anthropology (a 50-cent word for the study of human beings) than on theology (a 50-cent word for the study of God). For example, we think we have to pretend with God because of the games people play with each other. Because many of us are impressed with titles and status, we treat God like a stale pumpernickel loaf—trying to butter Him up by offering prayers laden with *thee* and *thou* and *mis*-pronunciations of His Hebrew names and titles. Some seem to think their prayers are more likely to reach heaven if spoken with a British accent.

Let me suggest that when you offer petitions with a fake British accent combined with a country twang, a southern drawl, Creole, Ebonics, or whatever they call those accents of the Northeast, you're just giving the Spirit another thing to sort out. The One who asked Moses, "Who made your mouth?" is not moved by eloquence of speech but by earnestness of heart. So save your Shakespearean theatrics for the next Broadway audition or church talent show.

He means it when He asks

Another game we play is asking one another "How are you?" as if we really want to know the answer. You might as well reply, "Fine," when someone asks how you're doing, because half the people don't care if you have problems and the other half are glad you have problems! Why not try your own informal study to verify those findings? Why not try telling someone how you're really doing rather than just saying "Fine"? You'll probably notice how they excuse themselves when you let them know you're facing some challenges. The results of our informal, independent studies usually confirm that the best policy is to mask how we're doing and be comforted by the artificial depth of our friends.

When we open up to people, we risk confronting the reality that most people are either (1) downright superficial and indifferent or (2) manipulative and seizing upon your vulnerabilities to profit from your predicaments or (3) so intoxicated by their own cocktail of pleasure and pain that they're numb to the needs of others.

God is the opposite of this. He seeks us out and tries to get us to open up, and most of the time it's not when things are going well. In fact, we see Him most active in human affairs when we are doing the worst. And the first thing He has to do in the conversation is get us to be honest with Him about our situation.

The first dialogue between God and humanity recorded in the Bible appears in Genesis 3 and takes place after Adam and Eve sinned (although we know they talked previously—see Genesis 1:28–30; 2:16–19). It was Adam and Eve who hid from God. He initiated conversation in the form of a question in order to get them to open up.

He knows you better than you know yourself

God likewise initiated conversation with Cain, trying to get him to think rationally before his anger toward Abel got out of control (Genesis 4). Even after Cain did what was unthinkable in the days before *Assassin's Creed* and *Grand Theft Auto*, God struck a plea-bargain with the world's first murderer. Although Cain fearfully sought escape from certain judgment rather than being sorry for his sinfulness, God's mercy prevailed over human ideas of justice.

God allowed Cain an open discourse and granted forbearance instead of throwing the book at him. No honest observer reading the account could say God is a vindictive, bloodthirsty Being. God seeks open communication and restoration whenever possible. We are the ones who conceal our true intents, thus cutting ourselves off from the help we desperately need. If God, having foreknowledge of the unrepentant hearts of men like Cain, still allowed lying tongues to wag without swift retribution, then there's no way He will decline the prayers of sincere seekers.

If you're convinced that you should open up and pray, yet hesitant because you don't know how, there's good news for you. No one else really knows either. The following insight is both humbling and encouraging: "The Spirit helps us in our weakness, for we do not know how we should pray, but the Spirit himself intercedes for us with inexpressible groanings" (Romans 8:26, *NET Bible*).

Think of the best public prayer you've ever heard. No matter how intense, ecstatic, eloquent, poetic, or intellectually stimulating it was—it wasn't good enough!

As I dwelt on that point, I was ambushed by the following question: "What if our distance from God's presence is measured by our pretense in prayer?" It's humbling for us as religious people to be told our prayers aren't as impressive to God as they are to us. Yet we are encouraged to know that the Holy Spirit reaches beyond our words to extract our deepest needs and desires and presents them to the throne on our behalf. The true power of prayer is not measured by how often God meets our demands but by how authentically and consistently we communicate with our Creator and Redeemer. Do your best to articulate the issues on your heart, and let Him do the rest.

Revived by a death wish

When doubt or guilt has dried out our prayer life and hindered us from talking with God about our true feelings, we can be strangely revived by the following prayers:

- "Why did I not perish at birth, and die as I came from the womb?" (Job 3:11).
- "My God, my God, why have you forsaken me? Why are you so far from saving me?" (Psalm 22:1).
- "I say to God my Rock . . . why must I go about mourning, oppressed by the enemy?" (Psalm 42:9).
- "Awake, Lord! Why do you sleep?" (Psalm 44:23).

These passages revive us not because they provide solutions for our problems or answers to satisfy our skepticism or promises to usher in a season of abundance. These texts simply grant us permission to stop hiding behind sanctimonious language when talking to God; permission to ask if He's paying attention to our plight; permission to question His administration of justice.

These verses were groans from the guts of men whom God boasted about. He commended one as "blameless and upright, a man who fears God" (Job 1:8), while the other was described as "a man after his [God's] own heart" (1 Samuel 13:14). Not only did God fail to chastise Job and David for these "irreverent" outbursts but He made their latter days better than their beginning.

If questioning God is blasphemous, why didn't God strike down David and Job rather than build them up? Since these men were not censured, isn't it reasonable to think that what may seem like insolent inquiries are actually God's way of encouraging us to provide full disclosure? The following quote confirms my take on this:

> *Keep your wants, your joys, your sorrows, your cares, and your fears before God.* You cannot burden Him; you cannot weary Him. He who numbers the hairs of your head is not indifferent to the wants of His children. . . . *Take to Him everything that perplexes the mind.* Nothing is too great for Him to bear, for He holds up worlds, He rules over all the affairs of the universe. Nothing that in any way concerns our peace is too small for Him to notice. *There is no chapter in our experience too dark for Him to read*; there is no perplexity too difficult for Him to unravel (*Peace Above the Storm*, 87–88, emphasis added).

Homicidal hyperbole

If you're turned off by narrow-minded zealots seeking to silence your questions instead of sympathizing with the pain that prompts your queries, cheer up—God is turned off by them too! A major subplot in the book of Job is grief ministry gone wrong. Job's friends were doing OK when they simply provided the ministry of presence and kept their mouths closed. However, after pondering his plight, they began offering Job some "constructive" criticism that quickly escalated to friendly fire.

The poet Kahlil Gibran says that "we speak when we cease to be at peace with our thoughts" and amplifies that profound statement by saying that "in much of our talking, thinking is half murdered" (*The Prophet*, 60). Job's friends eventually ceased to be at peace and felt it necessary to expound upon their speculative insights into his affliction. As they tormented Job (for his own good, they thought), their minds became casualties of their tongues. And later the "half-murdered" thinking of Eliphaz, Bildad, and Zophar almost got them killed (see Job 42:7–8). Posing as God's mouthpieces and presuming to know all the causes for Job's calamities, they overstepped their bounds and maligned the character of God.

Are questions safer than answers?

Is it possible that presuming to have all the answers is much more dangerous than daring to ask questions? Insincere men harassed Jesus with questions calculated to get Him to condemn Himself through His answers, yet He answered one after another. That doesn't mean Jesus always supplied the answers they were looking for. Christ frequently answered a question with a question. But He never asked questions like, "How dare you question me? Don't you know who I am?" Since Jesus took time to answer His enemies' questions, even though they were attempting entrapment, how can it be irreverent for His followers to ask Him questions if they're honestly seeking enlightenment or encouragement?

So ask your questions!

And when God answers, be sure to cover your mouth instead of your ears. Remember that He created your auditory transmitter and receptors with a 2:1 ratio. He gave us two ears and one mouth so that we can listen twice as much as we talk. If there is blasphemy in questioning God, it comes not so much from daring to ask but from neglecting to listen when He answers.

How do you know when He answers? Will it be audible, like talking to someone on the phone? That could happen very easily. There are several Bible apps for today's mobile devices that will read His word to you. Are you skeptical of God speaking through this old book we call the Bible?

> Only he who receives the Scriptures as the voice of God speaking to himself is a true learner. . . . God's holy, educating Spirit is in His word. A light, a new and precious light, shines forth from every page. Truth is there revealed, and words and sentences are made bright and appropriate for the occasion, as the voice of

God speaking to the soul (*Lessons of Love*, 19, 47).

As we've read here and there, we see that many Bible writers have already risked questioning God. His answers to them will help clarify the issues you're facing. We may feel trapped in our circumstances, like a motorist in a broken-down car on the shoulder of a dirt road during a snowstorm, but knowing other people have gotten stuck and survived gives us *hope* to survive. Knowing *how* they survived gives us *help* to survive. Here's a passage that reminds us we're not the first to question God and won't be the last.

> God speaks to us in His word. . . . Here is open before us the history of patriarchs and prophets and other holy men of old. They were men "subject to like passions as we are." James 5:17. We see how they struggled through discouragements like our own, how they fell under temptation as we have done, and yet took heart again and conquered through the grace of God. . . . As we read of the precious experiences granted them . . . the spirit that inspired them kindles a flame of holy emulation in our hearts (*Peace Above the Storm*, 76–77).

Director's cut

If we pay attention when we question God, we will discover that His answers often readjust our focus to show us a larger picture. This wide-angle lens will empower us to persevere through crises. Our eyes will be opened to see that the wicked aren't getting away with anything after all. Just because, sometimes, "sentence against an evil work is not executed speedily" (Ecclesiastes 8:11, KJV), it doesn't mean justice isn't served at all.

> As for me, my feet had almost stumbled; my steps had nearly slipped. For I was envious of the boastful, when

> I saw the prosperity of the wicked. . . . *Until I went into the sanctuary[1] of God*; then I understood their end. Surely You set them in slippery places; You cast them down to destruction. Oh, how they are brought to desolation, as in a moment! They are utterly consumed with terrors (Psalm 73:2–3, 17–19, NKJV, emphasis added).

You'll be disappointed but not devastated when your prayers for healing are overruled and your loved one dies. God will remind you that resurrection is a greater miracle than healing. He'll point out to you that your loved one is blessed with rest from their labors, and their works are remembered by Him even if forgotten by people (see Revelation 14:13; Ecclesiastes 2:15–17).

You will get a preview of your future eternal glory that will lighten your temporary affliction (see 2 Corinthians 4:17). A glimpse at what He's doing behind the set will have us asking, "Why didn't I see that?" or "Why didn't I understand?" The answer is simple. We're not God. If we could foresee and understand all the plot twists of life's narrative, it would be too much to handle. We would exclaim with David, "Such knowledge is a wonder greater than my powers; it is so high that I may not come near it" (Psalm 139:6, *Bible in Basic English*).

That's why Jesus said, "Don't ever worry about tomorrow. After all, tomorrow will worry about itself. Each day has enough trouble of its own" (Matthew 6:34, GW). Since Jesus said it's too much for us to worry ourselves over finite needs, then we need to trust Him with our cosmological concerns even more. It's hard to punctuate this point any better than the way we find it below:

---

1. For more insight on why reflecting on the sanctuary brought comfort and clarity to the Psalmist, I recommend the following resources: *Bible Readings for the Home*, vol. 1, pp. 174–184; *God Cares*, vol. 1, chapter 8, "God and His Sanctuary" and chapter 9, "God Schedules the Atonement"; *God Cares*, vol. 2, chapter 4, "God Reveals His Throne"; *Patriarchs and Prophets*, chapter 30, "The Tabernacle and Its Services"; *The Great Controversy*, chapter 23, "What Is the Sanctuary?" The authors prayerfully did their homework by comparing a wide array of commentaries and studies of the original languages but simplified the scholarly jargon for ordinary people to understand.

In the natural world we are constantly surrounded with mysteries that we cannot fathom. The very humblest forms of life present a problem that the wisest of philosophers is powerless to explain. Everywhere are wonders beyond our ken. Should we then be surprised to find that in the spiritual world also there are mysteries that we cannot fathom? *(Peace Above the Storm*, 107).

The biggest *why* of eternity!

Many of us respond, "I'll go along with that for now, but I'm gonna keep God busy for a couple of centuries when I see Him." Although we'll have all eternity to ask God the questions we've been filing away, my gut tells me we're going to forget most of them. And my gut is informed by someone with a sneak peek: "He will wipe all tears from their eyes, and there will be no more death, suffering, crying, or pain. These things of the past are gone forever" (Revelation 21:4, CEV).

In the end, the triumph of Christianity is not that Jesus provides logical answers for all our questions. It's a little like what I remember from my algebra classes. There were times when the assignment wasn't to solve the problem but to simplify it. Sometimes there are too many variables and insufficient information to solve the problem, so the best we can do with all our formulas is simplify it. First Corinthians 13:9 confirms the obvious—human knowledge is partial, and even prophecy provides only part of the puzzle. In other words, after the most intense prayer, study, and exercise of spiritual gifts, we still have to deal with variables that prevent us from solving all of life's problems.

There is a constant in life's equation, however. At Christ's return, all variables are eliminated. As 1 Corinthians 13:10 says, we learn "when that which is perfect has come, [and] then that which is in part will be done away" (NKJV). Although not all our curiosities are quenched either through study or divine revelation during this life, the future glory will bring an experience that makes you say, "What was I going to ask You about?" After our bodies are changed in that transformative twinkling of an eye (1 Corinthians 15:52) along with having our Father

14

wipe away all our tears (Revelation 21:4), I believe the biggest "why" question posed by eternity's guests will be, "Why didn't I trust Him more?"

2

Too Much to Handle

I'm sure you meant it from the bottom of your heart when you sought to comfort the bereaved—the parents whose teenager committed suicide; the couple whose baby died in the womb; the woman who found out that her husband lived a double life when his other wife and kids showed up at his funeral. I'm certain you were being as sympathetic as possible when you tried to reassure someone on the verge of eviction; when you were comforting that friend with an abusive spouse or that child suffering from abusive parents; or when you tried to encourage that struggling addict when you said:

"God never gives us more than we can handle."

Is that how it works? Do you mean if I weren't so strong, I wouldn't have been diagnosed with cancer while raising an autistic child? If I weren't so strong, my mom wouldn't have smoked crack while pregnant with me and let a man live with us who was more interested in me than her? If only I were weaker, then God would give me a pass on some of life's tragedies? If only I weren't so strong! If only I couldn't handle it, then my life would be so much more joyous!

Humpf! Am I the only one tired of "saints" offering religious Band-Aids to patch broken hearts and wounded spirits? Are you also weary of religious clichés that are supposed to comfort you? When will Christians learn that sentiments drawn from the shallow wells of overused platitudes aren't very saintly?

If one more well-meaning saint offers me the unsolicited assurance that "God won't put more on us than we can handle," I'm going to put something on them to handle. Where did that pithy attempt at sympathy come from, anyway? The Bible? Please! It's just another axiom that seems too wise to dispute because someone's preacher or their grandma or their preacher's grandma said it. Does anyone really believe that stuff when it's their turn to handle the pressure? More important, does the Bible really say that? Are we holding God responsible for something He didn't say?

Biblical blues

Did you know the Bible records some mighty men who teetered on the edge of suicidal tendencies? Did you know that Elijah and Moses prayed for God to take their lives because they felt their lot was more than they could handle? Did you know that contemplation of the cross even had Jesus depressed? Far from keeping a stiff upper lip, Jesus said His soul was "overwhelmed with sorrow to the point of death" (Matthew 26:38).

Christ's humanity was crushed by the demands of His divine mission. An angel was dispatched to Gethsemane to strengthen Jesus, for the weight of our sins had pressed upon the Savior until He lay like a wilted petal on the garden floor. On His way to Golgotha, Jesus had more placed upon Him than He could bear, making it necessary for Simon of Cyrene to tote the torturous instrument of our salvation.

The apostle Paul said that he didn't want the saints "to be ignorant about the suffering we experienced in the province of Asia. It was so extreme that it was beyond our ability to endure. We even wondered if we could go on living" (2 Corinthians 1:8, GW). Just as he didn't want the Thessalonians to be ignorant concerning those who sleep in Jesus (1 Thessalonians 4:13); just as he didn't want the Corinthians to be ignorant of spiritual gifts or of Satan's devices (1 Corinthians 12:1; 2 Corinthians 2:11); and just as he didn't want the Romans to be unaware of God's righteousness that comes through Christ's atoning sacrifice (Romans 10:3), Paul didn't want the church to be ignorant of his personal sufferings.

Why was it so important that Paul's audience know about his struggles? Was he seeking guests for a pity party? Not likely, since 2 Corinthians 1:4–6 tells us he had already received his comfort and wanted to share it. What does Paul's trouble two thousand years ago have to do with our trials of the twenty-first century?

For starters, Paul's testimony lets us know the Bible's authors weren't superheroes, immune to the weaknesses and temptations the rest of us face. Prophets and apostles didn't put on capes and fly over the commonplace stuff we have to wade through. They wrote to us as fellow strugglers. Sometimes they endured hard times and marched on as good soldiers, while failing and flailing on other occasions. All the heroes of the Bible were faulty (except Jesus), and many had times when they felt like giving up.

"That" clauses

Contrary to popular opinion, Paul stated from experience that God does sometimes allow more than we can handle. Problems will come too swiftly for us to dodge no matter how fast we are on our feet, and too big to bulldoze with the strongest willpower. Some may even undergo such pressure that death seems more appealing than life. Why? Could this depth of suffering serve any purpose? It may seem outrageous, but Paul teaches us that there are two main purposes behind God permitting these things to occur.[1]

Paul's teaching tool is the purpose clause. A purpose clause is used to take the mystery out of a person's actions by explaining motives. Purpose clauses answer the questions "Why?" and "For what reason or purpose?" The motivations are easily identified when signified by "in order that," as in the following verses:

> "He came for a testimony, in order that he might testify about the light, in order that all might believe through him" (John 1:7, literal translation from Greek).

Investigating motives in grammar isn't always easy, especially when

---

1. Permission is not the same as causation. God created us with freedom of choice, for love must be chosen, not forced. He also created us to be interdependent, meaning that our freedom of choice affects others. His ideal is that our choices would honor Him and show love for each other. Yet giving us the capacity to choose and therefore love involves risk on His part. My choice to drink alcohol may impair my judgment enough to believe I can safely drive home. Just as with drinks, one choice leads to another until my headlights are the last thing my victim sees. God's justice will hold me accountable for what my choices cost others. However, His grace is able to provide a sense of purpose out of tragedy. Maybe the survivors become activists to help curb deaths caused by DUI. This is difficult for the atheist to swallow. If evolving from an amoeba and living without moral absolutes provides a greater sense of purpose to suit his taste, God gives him the choice to chew on those implications.

translation is involved. Intentions are often hidden. Sometimes the clause is partially buried and all you see is the word *that*. In preparation for the strenuous job of digging into Paul's "that" clauses, let's warm up with a little Bible trivia.

Rats, rubber stamps, and psalm sandwiches

Do you know what the longest chapter of the Bible is? It probably didn't take long to answer, "Psalm 119." So let's see if you know what the shortest chapter of the Bible is. With just a little more effort, you probably discovered that it's Psalm 117. Do you know what the middle chapter of the Bible is? Yes, it's Psalm 118, sandwiched between the shortest and longest chapters.

Another gem of biblical trivia to impress your friends with is that the middle verse of the Bible is Psalm 118:8: "It is better to trust the Lord than to trust people" (NCV).

Would it surprise you to know the central text of the Bible is linked to the number-one reason for God giving us too much to handle? Where you place your trust determines your destiny, and one of the worst places to hang your trust is on your own ego. One of God's remedies for misplaced trust is *allowing burdens that outweigh our egos*. God sometimes allows more than we can handle so we'll stop handling it and hand it over. That's the message of the first "that" clause:

> For . . . we were pressed out of measure, above strength, insomuch that we despaired even of life: But we had the sentence of death in ourselves, *that we should not trust in ourselves*, but in God which raiseth the dead (2 Corinthians 1:8–9, KJV, emphasis added).

Not until we're stretched beyond our own abilities are we forced to trust others. And facing death really tests our trust in God's resurrection power. Paul had been a very self-sufficient person who still needed regular reminders to stay humble and dependent upon God (see 2 Corinthians 12:7–10; Galatians 1:14; Philippians 3:4–6). But isn't there a way to gauge our trust in God, short of having to go through life-threatening events?

Why not start by quizzing yourself? Is prayer your first resource or last resort? Do you acknowledge God in all your ways or depend on your own wisdom to direct your paths? Do you only seek His way after your path makes you feel like a rat in a maze, racing to the cheese that someone keeps moving? Do you ask God to set your agenda or bless it with a rubber stamp? No matter what your trust level is now, God gives you more exercises that will build it up.

Christ consciousness and ropes of sand

First we stretch our mouths open and admit that without Jesus we can do nothing (John 15:4–5). Any bricks in the building of trust not laid on this foundational statement will be swallowed in the swamps of self-deception, self-righteousness, self-condemnation, and self-destruction. That's not a popular sentiment in our age of self-help gurus. We like to be flattered with fluff like, "Dig deep for the treasure within, and you'll be rich in substance and spirit. Let your inner light, your innate Christ consciousness, be your guide."

If Christ's consciousness were innate (existing from birth) in humanity, He wouldn't have been crucified. Surely there would have been enough Christ-conscious people in the crowd to intervene, if such a thing were innate! What's innate is the civil war of the conscience. We know better without doing better. We do what we hate and hate ourselves for doing it (see Romans 7). After we submit to Christ, external things have no power to sever His connection with us (Romans 8). The greatest challenges we face are from within (James 1:13–15; 1 John 2:16). Don't be seduced by meditative practices that have us looking within instead of above (Jeremiah 17:9; Proverbs 28:26). The only power within that can bring positive change is the power to choose His help:

> Your promises and resolutions are like ropes of sand.
> You cannot control your thoughts, your impulses, your
> affections. The knowledge of your broken promises

and forfeited pledges weakens your confidence in your own sincerity, and causes you to feel that God cannot accept you; but you need not despair. What you need to understand is the true force of the will. This is the governing power in the nature of man, the power of decision, or of choice. . . . The power of choice God has given to men; it is theirs to exercise. You cannot change your heart, you cannot of yourself give to God its affections; but you can *choose* to serve Him. You can give Him your will; He will then work in you to will and to do according to His good pleasure (*Peace Above the Storm*, 42).

Tangible trust

After we've talked about ropes of sand, speaking about trust as something tangible may arouse our skepticism. We might think of trust as just a concept, but we exercise it in concrete ways. You sit on a chair because you trust it is strong enough to support your weight. It takes tremendous trust to drive down a narrow lane with only a strip of paint on the road guarding you from oncoming traffic. We exercise trust in our daily activities with such regularity that we've ceased to give them much thought.

God wants us to develop that level of unconscious trust with Him that we show when we drive to work without concentrating on every street name. He knows our trust can be easily diverted by the stuff He blesses us with. That's why He puts systems of tangible trust in place to keep our attention turned toward the Giver rather than the gift.

He did this first in Eden with the tree of the knowledge of good and evil. Unfortunately, Eve trusted the serpent's word instead of God's. She also chose to rely on her independent judgment to declare that the fruit was good for food, after God had said it would kill her (Genesis 3). Later in Genesis, we meet an imperfect man named Noah who trusted God by building the world's first ocean liner (Genesis 9:20-21; 6:8; Hebrews

11:7). The Hebrews had to show tangible trust to gain freedom from Egypt. Not through an armed revolution, though. God's plan seemed far less practical—eat a roasted lamb while standing in a house with the lamb's blood brushed around the doorpost (Exodus 12).

Because we commonly trust our treasures, God told us to return the tithe to show that we recognize everything is His. Since He blessed us with money to present an offering in the first place, we trust that He'll make the remainder of our funds more profitable than if we kept it all (see Jeremiah 48:7; Psalm 50:10–12; Proverbs 3:9–10; 23:4–5; Haggai 1:6–9; Malachi 3:8–12; Nehemiah 9:21).

We are prone to trust in our talents, hard work, and education, forgetting that it is only God's grace that gives us the power to get wealth. We also forget that the winner of the rat race is still a rat. That's why God commanded us to rest one day a week, so that we remember who we are and whose we are. Trust God over your boss and abilities, and then He'll work out your liberation, reputation, and prosperity while you worship (see 1 Timothy 6:17; Deuteronomy 8:17–18; 5:12–15; 4:5–7; Isaiah 58:13–14).

As you discover even more trust exercises, remember these aren't for the sake of earning God's favor but for you to evaluate your trust in His resources over your own. Because you've been routinely building trust during relatively easy times, you won't have to crack when the pressure becomes too much to handle.

Credible comforters

Paul's first purpose clause had to do with building trust in God, but this next one has to do with building others' trust in us. "You don't understand!" is the reflexive response of many hurting people toward well-intentioned sympathizers. However, they soften their tone and don't easily dismiss our efforts at comforting them when there's a shared experience. Preparing us to be credible comforters is the other reason Paul gives for God allowing more than we can handle:

Blessed be the God and Father of our Lord Jesus

Christ, the Father of mercies and God of all comfort, who comforts us in all our tribulation, [in order] that we may be able to comfort those who are in any trouble, with the comfort with which we ourselves are comforted by God (2 Corinthians 1:3–4, NKJV).

"That we may be able to comfort" could also be rendered "that we may have the power to comfort." The Greek word translated "able" is *dunamis*, from which we get the word *dynamite*, is often translated "power." Having the power to comfort others without having been comforted ourselves is like dynamite without nitroglycerin. The Christian's power to comfort others grows from our own cycles of calamity and comfort. This power disarms the defensive mechanisms of those who have been diagnosed, scammed, robbed of innocence, heartbroken, grief-stricken, and victimized.

To be a credible comforter means coming alongside of another rather than looking down in pity. We don't comfort from the outside looking in, as if standing behind protective glass. It isn't effective from a position of marching ahead, commanding the afflicted to keep up or pushing them from behind. To comfort others is like being in a three-legged race. You do your best to move as one, stride for stride. You have a vested interest in the success of the other because your destiny is tied to theirs. If they fall, you fall. If they fail, you fail. If they succeed, you succeed. You are going through it with them.

Heaven's economy is very efficient. God doesn't waste any of your experiences—they're recyclable. Sometimes what you are going through isn't for you but the people you need to witness to. Those who are called to full-time ministry should especially anticipate difficulties to press them without measure. How can we desire the depths of His consolation without having tribulations to expand the shallow channels of our selfish hearts? How do we rightly represent a sympathetic Savior when no suffering or sorrow has necessitated His sympathetic touch in our lives?

When we've soaked in suffering, we can sympathize more readily with the hardships of others—we can truly weep with those who weep. We are able to listen attentively, share just enough of our experience to let them know we have faced similar difficulties, and offer them the comfort that comforted us.

People are more trusting of a tour guide who has travelled the path before. It is our successful journey through the valley of the shadow of death that allows us to usher others through. Without such background, our approach to people in the shadows may cause them to think we're another stalker seeking to bring them into deeper darkness.

On the other hand, if you're singing "nobody knows the trouble I've seen," open your eyes and ears to the experience of others. Don't disqualify their attempts to comfort you; they may understand more than you know. All of us are like icebergs; we have more substance beneath the surface than meets the eye. Just as it may seem presumptuous for people to say they understand how you feel, it's presumptuous for you to deny the depth of their sorrows and their ability to identify. Be careful not to add self-righteousness to your self-pity.

Whenever you're tempted to think you're running alone, remember our Savior was acquainted with grief and tempted with situations like ours (see Hebrews 2:18; 4:15). He walked in our shoes—He lived in our skin. Jesus knew what it was like to feel exhaustion, abandonment, betrayal, anger, and sorrow. This common experience should inspire us with confidence in His ministry (Hebrews 2:14–18; 4:15–16).

When you look for that three-legged-race partner and see no one around, you can be confident that He's there beside you. Stay connected to Him, and He'll pick you up no matter how often you fall. He's not concerned about you slowing Him down either. He's not running scared through the valley, for He already conquered the forces of darkness.

Concrete comfort

By this we know love, because He laid down His life for us. And we also ought to lay down our lives for the brethren. But whoever has this world's goods, and sees his brother in need, and shuts up his heart from him, how does the love of God abide in him? My little children, let us not love in word or in tongue, but in deed and in truth (1 John 3:16–18, NKJV).

It's possible to give without loving, but it's impossible to love without giving. What good is it to tell a hungry person to be filled if you don't give them something to eat? How can we tell people to cheer up without ministering their emotional and spiritual needs?

Start with the humble ministry of presence, not seeking to make profound statements or pretending to have all the answers for their questions. Just be there. Sometimes people just want to know they're not alone. Sometimes they seclude themselves but secretly want someone to coax them out of their cave.

Job was initially glad for the presence of his friends but later called them miserable comforters. He let them know what they could do to help, but they seemed more interested in their self-righteous agendas than his dilemma. One of the things Job hoped for was prayer. When in all of their discussion did any of Job's friends say, "Let's pray to God about it"? They were later reprimanded because their clever sayings were false. They didn't have all the information but pretended to have all the answers. It's interesting that God didn't answer Job's questions nor tell any of the men the full story behind Job's suffering. God knew it all but didn't tell it all, and Job was still happy for His presence.

Next, look for an opportunity to find out your friend or family member's favorite scripture. If they don't have one, share a text that helped you through your difficult time and give a brief testimony. When it comes to praying with a fellow struggler, I usually don't ask if they would like prayer. I gently say, "Let me have a word of prayer with you before I go." I haven't had any objections to that approach. It's best to make the prayer short, using words that direct attention to the power of Jesus to overcome circumstances. It's important to leave right after "Amen." That way, you leave behind an atmosphere of prayer to encourage the person to keep that line of communication open.

What should be a commonsense question could lead to very concrete comfort for the bereaved. Does the grieving family need financial assistance? Any idea how much funerals cost today? Do you know whether there was a life insurance policy in place to take care of the expenses? Are there any special circumstances that annul the coverage, such as suicide? Was there a lengthy illness that already exhausted the person's finances? Don't wait for them to ask. Just anticipate the need and do what the Lord puts upon your heart.

Whenever I'm ministering in a bereavement setting, it is my conviction that clergy should bury their agendas and keep the family's wishes at the forefront. Honor their requests as long as there's no clear violation of Scripture, even if that's not what you would prefer. If someone does or doesn't want to be cremated, don't get upset with them. Remember that God wasn't dependent upon preexistent matter at Creation, and Christ won't be depending on our remains being arranged a certain way at the resurrection.

We must allow for personal and cultural expression in this area. For example Abraham went to great expense to bury his wife, Sarah, in a particular place. When Joseph neared death's door, he made a request regarding his bones, that they leave Egypt with his people's exodus. David baffled his friends when he fasted while his child was sick and ate after he died. Jesus honored the custom of anointing dead bodies when He commended Mary for anointing him before His death.

The most unusual arrangement I ever heard of was for James Henry Smith, an avid Pittsburg Steelers fan. He received a traditional burial in a casket on the day of his funeral, but the viewing on the night before was a different story. His family and funeral home arranged for him to be placed in his favorite recliner rather than a coffin. Not only was he dressed from head to toe in Steelers clothing and memorabilia but was surrounded by it as well. As if that weren't enough, they rounded out the set with a TV playing continuous loops of Steelers highlights. His beer and cigarettes were right by his side as though he were watching the game.

Whether Smith's story amuses or disgusts you, remember that funerals are about culture and legacy. Rather than debating the virtues and vices of Smith's viewing, it would be more profitable to dwell on what we want our legacy and destiny to be. If you died today and the people close to you arranged your body in the middle of your favorite things, what would the scene look like? Would your valuables be more enduring than jerseys, beer, and cigarettes? It's not only a question of what you want to be remembered for but where you want to meet your friends again. They'll be better able to handle your death if they know they have an opportunity for a heavenly future with you.

3

Yell at God and Live

Have you ever basked in the sunlight beneath blue skies, while the weather of your soul blacked out heaven's rays? Has sorrow reduced your reservoir of tears to a salty residue of evaporated anguish? Have you ever sobbed till your body continued in the motions even after your emotions ebbed? Has tragedy, regret, or betrayal carved out your insides, leaving your heart hollow? Do you wonder if your groans are whisked away in the wind before reaching heaven? Or perhaps they're gurgling past God's throne as indistinguishable droplets in the babbling river of human lamentations? Has your frustration with your Father led you to imagine yourself shaking your fist in His face for abandoning you in this asylum? Have you ever taken it the next step and glared into the sky to unload a full-throated barrage of blame at God?

If you're like me, after you did it, you stood back waiting for black clouds to engulf you; the loudest thunderclap of your life to deafen you; and then a jolt of divine vengeance to ignite you!

God in His mercy, instead of killing me instantly for my insolence, called me to ministry. Instead of cursing Him and dying, I yelled at God and lived . . . to write about it.

Biblical blasphemy

How can an ordained minister have the audacity to suggest such blasphemy? I read it in the Bible. Perhaps you've never read the passage before, or never paused long enough to consider its implications because it scared you too much. Here it is in its entirety. Selah—pause and think about it.

> O Lord God who delivers me!
> By day I cry out and at night I pray before you.
> Listen to my prayer!
> Pay attention to my cry for help!

For my life is filled with troubles and I am ready to enter Sheol.

They treat me like those who descend into the grave.

I am like a helpless man, adrift among the dead, like corpses lying in the grave, whom you remember no more, and who are cut off from your power.

You place me in the lowest regions of the Pit, in the dark places, in the watery depths.

Your anger bears down on me, and you overwhelm me with all your waves. (Selah)

You cause those who know me to keep their distance; you make me an appalling sight to them.

I am trapped and cannot get free.

My eyes grow weak because of oppression.

I call out to you, O Lord, all day long; I spread out my hands in prayer to you.

Do you accomplish amazing things for the dead?

Do the departed spirits rise up and give you thanks? (Selah)

Is your loyal love proclaimed in the grave, or your faithfulness in the place of the dead?

Are your amazing deeds experienced in the dark region, or your deliverance in the land of oblivion?

As for me, I cry out to you, O Lord; in the morning my prayer confronts you.

O Lord, why do you reject me, and pay no attention to me?

I am oppressed and have been on the verge of death since my youth.

I have been subjected to your horrors and am numb with pain.

Your anger overwhelms me; your terrors destroy me.

They surround me like water all day long; they join forces and encircle me.

You cause my friends and neighbors to keep their distance; those who know me leave me alone in the darkness (Psalm 88, *NET* Bible).

Always consider the source

The first important fact about this psalm doesn't concern the lyrics but rather the psalmist—a highly privileged sacred-song writer. Heman was appointed by the Levites, Israel's priestly class, to be in charge of the music, and he worked under the supervision of King David (see 1 Chronicles 15:17; 25:6). Asaph, another notable psalmist, served as Heman's associate—his right-hand man (1 Chronicles 6:39). Ethan, another headliner in the book of Psalms, is listed as Heman's left-hand man (1 Chronicles 6:44).

Heman's musical ministry spanned from when the ark of the covenant returned from the Philistines down to the building of the temple during Solomon's reign. Heman's work was so commendable that his sons were appointed to succeed him (1 Chronicles 25:1). "All these were sons of Heman the king's seer [prophet]. They were given him through the promises of God to exalt him. God gave Heman fourteen sons and three daughters" (1 Chronicles 25:5).

Isn't it amazing how someone could have all the trappings of success and still feel like a failure? Heman was honored by his peers and superiors. He was a composer, vocalist, multi-instrumentalist, administrator, and prophet. Having seventeen children was enough to secure unquestionable bragging rights in those days (Psalm 127:3). When your offspring are publically recognized as a fulfillment of God's promises to exalt you, then you can really stick your chest out! How could Heman ever feel lonely when he and his wife were multiplying like rabbits and multitudes were praising his private and public successes?

We don't know all the details leading to Heman's fame, why God exalted him so highly, or what circumstances pressed him so low. However, we know that nothing we accumulate or accomplish in life provides insurance against adversity. You may have heard it said that a testimony never comes without a test. Beware of coveting someone else's testimony when you're ignorant of the tests they face.

Heman's tests were so critical that they induced him to blame God for his problems. Of course, blunt descriptions of dismal circumstances aren't unusual in the Psalms. Many of them begin with weeping that endures through the night but climax with joy in the morning. What's different here? Psalm 88 is the reversal of that pattern. It goes from bad to worse, from questioning God to blaming Him. What could prompt a man of God to write a song that moves from suspecting God of neglect to accusing Him of abuse? How did Heman write such poetic negativity without suffering God's swift and stern judgment? How did he publish it without suffering human censorship?

The only bright spot is in the first verse of the passage, when he refers to the Lord God "who delivers me!" Nothing seems positive after that point. No apology. No resolution. No praise. No hopeful promises. Instead we see a continual seeking of sympathy, pleading for answers, and blaming God. He blames God for everything—rejecting his prayers, physically afflicting him, emotionally abusing him, and alienating him from friends and family.

Apparently he's writing during his mature years, since he's reflecting on how he's suffered depression from his youth. If God allowed an older man such liberty of expression, shouldn't we be patient when dealing with the mood swings common in younger years?

Heman's view of God as the source of His pain while he stubbornly cried out to God for help is reminiscent of Job's declaration, "Though he slay me, yet will I hope in him" (Job 13:15). Both men seemed to reason, "No matter how I try to make things better, they get worse. As much as I hate to think it, nobody but God is wise and powerful enough to orchestrate this chaos. If God is my assailant, no one but Him can rescue me. In spite of my feelings, I must continue to seek Him."

You I make me sick!

Heman knows that the most persuasive argument to present to God is his own great need. He knows where his help comes from, if he's going to get any help at all. How can he state his case if his head overrules his heart's plea to clearly portray its distress? Does the 911 operator dispatch emergency assistance to people who call to have casual conversation? Does the doctor provide aggressive medical treatment for someone who says their symptoms are mild? Medical professionals routinely deliver life-saving treatment in an even-tempered manner to people ranting hysterically at them. Don't you think God's "skin" is thick enough to deal with our outbursts triggered by the duress of living in a sinful environment?

In spite of our best efforts to remain sweet and sunny, respectful and reverent, pious and polite, we are tempted and sometimes succumb to petulance, bitterness, and rebelliousness. We break taboos, if nowhere else than in our thoughts. We want to be righteous but find ourselves bound by secrets and regrets. We've told everyone but God, only to be disappointed by lack of concern or confidentiality. Perhaps we haven't told God or anyone else. We just keep cramming our pain down as far as it will go and trying to keep a lid on it. But every time we break the seal to cram some new stuff, some old stuff escapes. Sometimes it oozes. Sometimes it surges. Sometimes it erupts. No matter how it escapes, it is evidence that we are no match for the pressure of this world.

One of my mentors, E .E. Cleveland, used to say, "Impression without expression leads to depression." Some of us are making ourselves sick by not finding a healthy way to express our stress. That's not spurious pop psychology or Eastern mysticism. Modern research is verifying the following insight:

> The relation that exists between the mind and the body is very intimate. When one is affected, the other sympathizes. The condition of the mind affects the health to a far greater degree than many realize. Many diseases from which men suffer are the result of mental depression. Grief, anxiety, discontent, remorse, guilt, distrust, all tend to break down the life forces and to invite decay and death (*Pathways to Health and Happiness*, 77).

Collateral damage

We're not the only ones who suffer when we're too pious to release our pressurized emotions toward God. It hurts those around us, especially those closest to us. Not simply because they're concerned about us, but because they're concerned about themselves. When we don't express the pain of our loneliness to the Lord, then it gets expressed to others in ways that perpetuate our loneliness. Why? How? We've made ourselves too difficult to be around.

Some say misery loves company but that kind of love is a one-way street to a dead end. Just as flies contaminate everything they touch with regurgitated manure, miserable people rehearse real and imaginary difficulties until everyone is affected. Or should I say infected? And what is the typical reaction to flies?

The tragic results of not telling God about our problems are seen in people like Cain (Genesis 4). God saw that Cain's anger management strategies weren't working and sought to preempt the world's first murder by reasoning with him. Cain was angry with God for rejecting his offering but showing favor to his brother Abel's sacrifice. Instead of admitting to God that he had a problem, he took out his frustration by killing his brother. Abel wasn't the source of Cain's problem, and getting rid of him didn't resolve Cain's issues. Most of us wouldn't dream of taking things that far, but Jesus said we don't have to commit exactly the same crime to share Cain's condemnation:

> You have heard that the ancients were told, "You shall not commit murder" and "Whoever commits murder shall be liable to the court." But I say to you that everyone who is angry with his brother shall be guilty before the court; and whoever says to his brother, "You good-for-nothing," shall be guilty before the supreme court; and whoever says, "You fool," shall be guilty enough to go into the fiery hell (Matthew 5:21–22, NASB).

Venting on one another has both temporal and eternal consequences. God is able to forgive our angry outbursts, but our friends and family will have a hard time forgetting. God grants second chances, but your employer might not. Since our stuff is going to come out one way or another and is too hazardous for humans to safely handle, then why not take it to God?

Prayer is the safest pressure valve to release whatever's boiling inside of us, and His word is the best anger extinguisher there is. That's one reason Psalm 88 is in the Bible. It gives us an example of an upright man who was down on life and God. Heman felt alone, but God was still with him, granting him breath to blame and the talent to musically articulate his agony. He felt cursed even though he was surrounded by evidence of God's blessings. He complained to God, argued with God, yelled at God—yet he lived. He lived because he maintained his connection with the Source of Life.

Passion week parallel

If God's blessing on Heman's life isn't enough to prove God's sympathy and patience, then take another look at the life and death of Christ. Especially note the last week of His public ministry. "Passion Week" is an apt name for the spectrum of emotions flooding the Savior's heart as He approached the cross. Christ's experience that week paralleled the distress of Psalm 88.

It started on a triumphant note, when Jesus rode toward Jerusalem like a king and was greeted by a palm-branch parade. Just outside the city, He puzzled everyone by abruptly bursting into a crying spell that halted the parade. Shortly after that, He rampaged through the temple, casting out the moneychangers. And then, the disciples couldn't make rhyme or reason out of His cursing a fig tree that shriveled up and died in response to His usually life-giving word.

Jesus drifted into loneliness despite being surrounded by His friends at His last Passover fellowship. His countenance sank as He anticipated the cross He would bear. He longed for prayer partners to encourage Him as He lifted the cup of God's wrath to His lips. However, even His bold inner circle of Peter, James, and John couldn't stay awake. All His disciples fled when He was arrested. One was so anxious to escape that he ran right out of his clothes (Mark 14:51–52).

The downward spiral continued as Christ was beaten and spit upon by the people He created. Priests fabricated such ridiculous charges that the pagan governor Pilate rebuked them for not having a good reason to bring Jesus to court. The Savior suffered the taunts of crooked Herod, who entertained himself by having Jesus beaten when He refused to work a miracle for him. Even the two criminals being crucified on both sides of him insulted and taunted Christ. Isn't it amazing that even when people are in a hopeless situation, they seek to elevate themselves by putting others down? Jesus absorbed all the slander and abuse hurled at Him and still prayed, "Father, forgive them; for they know not what they do" (Luke 23:34, KJV).

Heavenly angels were amazed and appalled at the scene. I imagine them asking, "How is it they don't know what they're doing? How much evidence do they need?" Earth is fortunate for the restraint of the Father upon the angels that kept them from storming this planet. Just one angel could have brought bloody retribution to all the guilty parties in the region, and I bet the angels were itching to wage a holy war against humanity (see 2 Kings 19:35).

However, God was waging war at a higher level than any of His hosts could comprehend. They had to obey His order to stand down. The Son was using the unconventional weapon of sacrificial love. He laid down His life as a substitution to save those who hate Him. He didn't come only to identify with the woe we experience in this life but also to identify with the sin at the root of it all. He tasted the ordinary travail of this world as well as the wrath of a holy God described as a consuming fire (Hebrews 12:29). He suffered the penalty for every sin and sinner since the dawn of disobedience. Although Christ is acquainted with our pain, we can never fully comprehend His.

Jesus yelled

The internal struggle of He who knew no sin to become identified with sin brought a disturbing cry from His lips, never heard before or since. All that tormented Heman's heart and ours, in addition to the terrors that await unrepentant sinners, was upon Christ's heart as He "cried with a loud voice, Eli, Eli, lama sabachthani?—that is, My God, My God, why have You abandoned Me [leaving Me helpless, forsaking and failing Me in My need]?" (Matthew 27:46, AMP).

Jesus yelled at God and died—yet He lives. Because He lives, we can live, even though our thoughts, words, and deeds deserve otherwise. In light of what He already endured on our behalf, what more can be inflicted on Him? He's taken the worst we could dish out.

Every problem for which we seek a solution pales in comparison to the sin problem and its sacrificial solution. Every complaint that we could lodge against the Lord has already been anticipated and answered on the cross. He has demonstrated His understanding of our perplexities. He has shown His willingness to empty heaven to save us.

Trade piece for peace

How do we receive what He has to offer? Start by emulating Heman's example and presenting our great need before God without holding back. Share what's really on our minds, rather than what we think He wants to hear. He knows us better than we know ourselves, so why try to fool Him (see Psalm 139)?

Many of Hollywood's stars get their shine from make-up artists, plastic surgeons, PR specialists, borrowed jewelry, and substance abuse. We're sometimes shocked when we see paparazzi photos of them without makeup and designer clothes. But God is never shocked by superficial spirituality.

God's not encouraging you to open up because He needs the information. He already has it. He wants us to remove our masks so we can see ourselves. Bargain with Him, cry and yell if that's what it takes to begin with. After you see yourself in the mirror of God's word and accept the transforming power of His love, He'll give you a peace of mind that decreases your need to give Him a piece of your mind.

4

Jesus Wept

He wasn't a gang-banger, drug dealer, addict, or womanizer, reaping the consequences of a self-destructive lifestyle. He defied the stereotypes some people have of young black males by excelling in academics, being as active in church as in athletics, and helping his single mother with the younger children. The dimples that accented his charming smile seemed like God's signature upon a masterpiece. How could Chancellor die at fourteen of "natural causes"?

Whether it made sense or was fair or not, I was assisting at my nephew's funeral. If there ever was an occasion for weeping, this certainly qualified. Yet why do people of faith seem compelled to show their strength by holding back their tears? Doesn't the Bible say that Jesus *wept* (John 11:35)?

Jesus held nothing back in expressing His sorrow. "He is despised and rejected of men; *a man of sorrows, and acquainted with grief*" (Isaiah 53:3). "And when he was come near, he beheld the city, and wept over it" (Luke 19:41). "Then he said to them, 'My soul is overwhelmed with sorrow to the point of death' " (Matthew 26:38). "Being in anguish, he prayed more earnestly, and his sweat was like drops of blood falling to the ground" (Luke 22:44). "During the days of Jesus' life on earth, he offered up prayers and petitions with fervent cries and tears to the one who could save him from death" (Hebrews 5:7).

The Bible says lots that honest people don't like. These particular verses are problematic for some. What kind of Savior is this? A crybaby, mama's boy, creampuff, milksop, sissy, punk, wimp, wuss? How can Jesus see to wipe away the tears from our eyes if He can't dam up His own ducts? If weeping signified weakness, how could Jesus be our burden bearer, strong tower, refuge in time of trouble? If Jesus *is* strong and masculine, then how can weeping be synonymous with weakness?

Weeping not a sign of weakness

When blue-collar guys encountered Jesus and they shook His calloused hand, they knew He was one of them. Years of carpentry earned Him credibility with the working class that study alone could never accomplish. We don't know that Jesus was a physically imposing figure, but we do know there was a commanding presence about Him. He single-handedly flipped over the money-changers' tables, opened their money bags and cast their currency to the ground, ran off the animal traders' livestock, and made these men feel so lucky to get away alive that none of them stopped to pick up their money (see John 2:13–17; Mark 11:15–17).

His work ethic, strength of character, and courage to confront evil lent a persuasive power to Christ's words. "Follow me," was Jesus' two-word ultimatum that handily pried a businessman away from his profits (Luke 5:27–28). The same two-word command arrested the attention of four burly men with backs broadened from rowing boats and straining at fishing nets (Mark 1:16–20). Again, this is the same Jesus who spoke with so much conviction and eloquence that armed soldiers who were sent to arrest Him reported they were powerless to do so, because "no one ever spoke the way this man does" (John 7:46). Strong men don't follow weak men. Laborers have little tolerance for mere talkers. Soldiers only acquiesce to those in authority. The power of Christ's words to persuade men refutes the notion of a teddy-bear Messiah that's sometimes promoted.

Even greater than the ability of Christ's words to "win friends and influence people" was their healing power. He came across a man who had been blind from birth and, after putting mud on his eyes, spoke *seven words* to restore his sight: " 'Go, wash in the Pool of Siloam' " (John 9:7, KJV). One day He worked a wholesale healing by using only *six words* to heal ten men of leprosy: "Go, show yourselves to the priests" (Luke 17:14). For a man paralyzed by guilt as well as disease, Jesus brought healing with *five words*: "Friend, your sins are forgiven" (Luke 5:20). "Stretch out your hand," was the *four-word* command that restored a man's withered digits (Mark 3:5). Jesus tamed a tempest that terrified His disciples with a *trio* of words: "Quiet! Be still!" (Mark 4:39). "Be opened" were the *two words* Jesus spoke to heal a man who couldn't hear or talk (Mark 7:34). A legion of demons had to flee when Jesus gave them a *one-word* directive, "Go!" (Matthew 8:32). If Jesus had starred in *The Exorcist*, it would have been a commercial instead of a movie.

When a man with dominion over demons and disease can break down and cry, I conclude that tears don't automatically make a man effeminate. If we add other bold men of the Bible, we end up with quite a list of tough guys who shed tears. David the giant-killing warrior-king wept. Joseph, who was strong enough to resist sexual temptation during a lonely time of life and had the power to forgive his brothers' betrayal, wept. Nehemiah, skillful and strong enough to use carpenter tools in one hand and wield a sword in the other, wept. If you've ever succumbed to weeping, you're in strong company.

Weeping is not a denial of faith

Imagine the initial response to Jesus' nonchalant affirmation that Lazarus' condition was not for death but for the glory of God (John 11:1–5). Mary, Martha, and Lazarus must have rejoiced with great expectation of the miraculous breakthrough that would occur momentarily.

Theirs was a home where Jesus could rest His dusty feet and relax His mind. They were faithful to Him no matter the ebb and flow of popular opinion. It was refreshing for the Master to speak freely to an audience without anyone seeking to trap Him with His words. It was a break from the formal settings of the pretentious religious leaders. These hosts didn't mind if Jesus chose to put His elbows on the table or lick His fingers while eating Martha's greens and cornbread.

This close-knit family had witnessed Jesus healing people by touching them and by being touched by them. They saw Him gaze directly into the eyes of the diseased as He commanded healing and wholeness to replace brokenness. They also knew of those He healed without ever visiting them. Some had been strangers who learned to believe in a benefactor they never met. With such a precedent of power demonstrated on casual acquaintances, their hearts hummed with blessed assurance of what He would do for His close friends.

But minutes began to feel like hours, and they started having questions. Did the messenger forget to relay instructions they must comply with? Should Lazarus stand up and roll up his mat? Should they take him to the pool of Bethesda? Should he dip in the Jordan River seven times?

I wonder how many times they rehearsed the promise that Lazarus' sickness was not unto death. This statement became painfully puzzling as their hope was enveloped by Hades. I can hear Mary sobbing, "I thought he wasn't sick unto death." I can feel Martha's frustration: "How was God glorified while my brother trembled with fever and moaned in pain?" I can hear Lazarus gasping, "Not . . . unto . . . death . . . glory . . . to . . . God." Suddenly his chest rises no more.

Confusion also arose in the minds of the twelve disciples when Jesus said He was going to wake up Lazarus. His relaxed tone led the disciples to believe Lazarus was on the mend, not in the grave. No one spoke of waking up dead people.

The faith of His closest friends and followers was put to the test. Had they forgotten He'd already raised some from the dead (Luke 7:11–17; 8:49–56)? Did they remember when He said He had power to lay down His own life and take it up again (John 10:17–18)? Did they believe what He said He would do at the last day?

> Now this is the will of the one who sent me—that I should not lose one person of every one he has given me, but raise them all up at the last day. For this is the will of my Father—for everyone who looks on the Son and believes in him to have eternal life, and I will raise him up at the last day. . . . No one can come to me unless the Father who sent me draws him, and I will raise him up at the last day. . . .
>
> The one who eats my flesh and drinks my blood has eternal life, and I will raise him up on the last day" (John 6:39-40, 44, 54, *NET Bible*).

Mary and Martha were confident His presence would have prevented their brother's death. Both said, "Lord, if you had been here, my brother would not have died" (John 11:21, 32, *NET Bible*). Martha expressed her belief that Lazarus would live again at the last day, so she had been paying attention to His earlier teaching. Mary is noted for her love of learning at Jesus' feet as if to prevent His words from falling to the floor (Luke 10:38–42). If Martha had opportunity to learn that the consummation of eternal life occurs at the resurrection on the last day, we can be sure Mary shared in that hope.

These sorrowful sisters had been inspired by the Messiah's promise that when their eyelids yielded to the sleep of death, they would be awakened by His voice and arise from their earthen beds (John 5:25–29). But knowledge and hope didn't eliminate the hurt for them, any more than they do today. God's promises don't anesthetize our pain, making us believe that everything's OK when it's not.

Christianity doesn't demand the denial of reality, saying that our difficulties are illusions. Just as a broken arm is real, so is a broken heart. Both take time to heal and require exercise to recover their ability to function. We must be still and know that God is healing in imperceptible ways on the one hand, and exercise active faith in His promises on the other. This balance requires clear thinking. The anesthetic fog of drugs and alcohol, the quick fixes of short-term relationships, or the delusional concepts of Eastern philosophies will only worsen a fractured state of mind.

Jesus didn't come seeking enlightenment, for He is "the true light that enlightens everyone" (John 1:9, WEB). Jesus was fully aware of His identity, position, mission, and power. He knew that as the author of life He had authority over death; and yet He wept. He knew He had a solution to human suffering that doesn't include innumerable deaths and rebirths before one reaches paradise. Christ's public prayer at the grave of Lazarus (John 11:41-42) served as an announcement that the Father had already answered His private prayer; and yet He wept. God was going to be glorified, but not through healing. He had something even greater in store. Lazarus was privileged with being raised from the grave after four days of death. If our situation worsens after we tell it to Jesus, He's possibly setting us up for record-breaking glorification. And yet we weep.

Since Jesus wept while constantly confirming His foreknowledge and abilities, it is impossible for weeping to signify a lack of faith. If His most devoted followers affirmed their faith in the Savior's power while choking back tears, then we can be faithful and weep too.

Now that we know Christians have liberty to lament, the question still lingers, "If weeping isn't a sign of weakness or lack of faith, then why did Jesus weep?"

Jesus wept *with* the people

" 'My dwelling place will be with them; I will be their God, and they will be my people' " (Ezekiel 37:27). "We are the temple of the living God. As God has said: 'I will live with them and walk among them, and I will be their God, and they will be my people' " (2 Corinthians 6:16). "I will put my laws in their minds and write them on their hearts. I will be their God, and they will be my people" (Hebrews 8:10). "Behold, the tabernacle of God is with men, and he will dwell with them, and they shall be his people, and God himself shall be with them, and be their God" (Revelation 21:3, KJV).

It's been said that we need to pay special attention when God repeats Himself. So what's His point in repeating the promise that He will dwell with us and be our God? The life of Jesus demonstrated to us that even though God is transcendent, He is also intimate with us. God's position above the world does not detract from His sympathy for the world. He's not the impersonal, rationalistic God of the Deists, spinning worlds into orbit to be ruled by laws so unalterable that even He would not dare intervene using miracles.

Our Father is not like most of the pagan gods, whose intimacy with human beings (according to legend) was laced with lust. The gods didn't interact with people to impart grace but to engage in self-indulgence at the cost of their subjects. The tales of Zeus often portray him as seducing women, which resulted in their destruction at the hands of his jealous wife, Hera. What appetite did he subdue or which comfort did he deny himself in order to have experiential knowledge of human suffering? What plan did he ever propose for humans to dwell with him on Mount Olympus?

Our Creator enjoyed the company of His crowning work from the beginning. Adam and Eve had direct conversation with God without being afraid. Even after they exchanged this privilege for a piece of forbidden fruit, God demonstrated His compassion by clothing their shame. Before the death sentence was announced, deliverance was proclaimed. Before sin ruptured their relationship, a sacrifice had been prepared to bring restoration. Since humanity has become too sinful and self-absorbed to desire or even sense God's presence, He develops ways to get our attention in advance of our needs.

God pulled out all the stops to get the attention of Pharaoh, as well as the Hebrews, en route to the Exodus: He turned rods into snakes, the Nile into blood, dust into lice, etc. God's purpose in liberating the oppressed from forced labor was to grant them freedom to worship Him, serve Him, *dwell* with Him. That's why it wasn't long before Moses was directed to build a tabernacle, or tent of meeting, where God could dwell with His people. Designing a mobile meeting place was His way of assuring the Israelites they were never alone. Unlike other gods, His presence wasn't limited to one location.

The Israelites were privileged to have the prophetic family of Moses, Miriam, and Aaron to communicate God's will, but God wanted the people to know there was also a place where they could meet Him for themselves. Although God established a priesthood for the nation, the nation itself was to be a priesthood also (see Exodus 19:6). Although God gave the Ten Commandments to Moses on tables of stone, His goal was for the Holy Spirit to write those laws on the people's hearts (Jeremiah 31:22; Ezekiel 11:19–20). Even though God awakened prophets early in the morning to make His will known, His goal was for His Spirit to speak directly to us throughout the day (Jeremiah 7:25; Isaiah 30:21; 59:21; Matthew 10:19–20). God always aimed to get as close to His people as possible. He was determined to experience our joys and sorrows as well as to share His triumphant love with us.

The apostle John efficiently encapsulated God's desire for closeness with His creation when he wrote, "The Word was made flesh, and dwelt among us" (John 1:14, KJV). This is such a concise declaration that our modern English language is slow to grasp the significance. The word translated "dwelt" is derived from the word for "tabernacle." Moses' tent of meeting was made of things like badger skins, but in Christ, God tabernacled with us in a tent of human flesh. Jesus was the ultimate mobile meeting place. Emmanuel, "God with us," could finally feel firsthand what we experience in this world. He lived without shielding Himself from hardship so that none could say He doesn't understand or care. He rejoiced with those who rejoice when He turned water into wine at a wedding party (John 2). Now He weeps with those who weep on the way to Lazarus' tomb.

Jesus was so connected to humanity that He identified with Mary's and Martha's pain to the point of weeping, yet so connected with heaven that He confidently commanded Lazarus to come forth. It is because He has walked in our sandals that the Father has committed all judgment to Jesus (John 5:22; 2 Corinthians 5:10). He wept bitterly as He interceded for us on earth and continues to intercede for us in heaven (Hebrews 4:15; 5:7–9; Romans 8:34). If anyone is lost, it's not because the Judge isn't sympathetic to our situation. If His verdict prevents us from entering the kingdom, it's not because we don't have a good Lawyer to argue our case. Jesus is both Judge and Advocate (or Lawyer if you please). He understands human nature from the inside out with all of its weaknesses, and He demonstrated how we may overcome.

When the trumpet blows at the end of this world, those sleeping in Jesus will be reunited with those alive in Christ as they rise to meet the Savior in the clouds (1 Thessalonians 4:13–18). When the redeemed receive their reward and sin is eradicated, we will dwell in ceaseless joy with Jesus. When God wipes away all our tears and death has died, Christ won't have anyone to cry with anymore (Revelation 21:4; 20:14). But as long as "people are destined to die once" (Hebrews 9:27), Jesus will dwell with the grieving and weep with those who weep.

Jesus wept *for* the people

"Lazarus is dead. And I am glad for your sakes that I was not there, that you may believe" (John 11:14–15, NKJV). So Jesus was *glad* He wasn't there to prevent Lazarus' death? Maybe the translators made a mistake? No. This is indeed the same Greek word Jesus used to describe how the shepherd "*rejoices* more over that [one lost] sheep than over the ninety-nine that did not go astray" (Matthew 18:13, KJV). This is the same word Jesus used when He interrupted the disciples' victory lap to redirect their enthusiasm: "Do not rejoice that the spirits submit to you, but rejoice that your names are written in heaven" (Luke 10:20). This is the same word describing how Zaccheus "received Him *joyfully*" (Luke 19:6) when Jesus invited Himself to the tax man's house.

"Is He glad that Lazarus is dead, so that we may believe?" one disciple whispers.

"Is He still upset that we couldn't cast out that demon?" another questions.

"It doesn't seem to pay to be His friend. Remember what happened to John the Baptist? Now Lazarus. Who's next?" questions someone else.

"Shhhh, you know how good His hearing is!" warns another.

The disciples' state of unbelief must have been quite deplorable to warrant such a deadly delay. And this passage has me wondering whether there's someone waiting on me to be more faithful so that their prayers can be answered. It's disturbing to think that Jesus would let one person's unbelief bring suffering upon another. Even more disturbing is that the twelve frequently received personal tutoring after Jesus dismissed the crowds but *still* had so little faith. How could they have healed people and cast out demons and yet have such abysmal faith that the Messiah would feel a need to use such extreme measures? How could they respond to His announcements that He would soon be crucified with arguments about whom was the greatest among them (Mark 9:31–34; 10:32–45)?

Unbelief brings more sorrow to Jesus than anything else. It inhibits His ability to alleviate suffering and provide the comfort we seek (see Matthew 13:58; Mark 6:5–6). Jesus wept for His disciples because He could see ahead to the garden, when their self-sufficiency had them sleeping instead of praying (Mark 14:37–40). He wept for them because they didn't believe His warnings of how seriously their faith would be shaken (see Luke 22:31; Matthew 26:31). Jesus wept for them because He knew that Judas' conspiracy with the priests was the final stroke that would cut him off from grace. Jesus wept for the shame His most vocal spokesman would feel after denying Him three times (Matthew 26:69–75).

Jesus' raising Lazarus after he'd been dead four days was meant to build the disciples' faith, so that they would anticipate Christ's resurrection on the third day. If they had learned from this miracle, they wouldn't have been terrified after He was crucified. They wouldn't have doubted the reports of His resurrection. His heart ached for them, yearning to overcome their skepticism and spare them unnecessary anguish.

Jesus wept because raising Lazarus wouldn't have a strong enough impact to inoculate them against despair when He died. Their sluggish faith and swift forgetfulness prevented them from being comforted by this preview of His own resurrection.

Jesus wept and weeps today for the multitudes that reject Him no matter what He says or does. He discerns the consequences that will overtake those who won't trust Him. He grieves for people who resist every merciful call to repentance and eternal life. He sorrowed that some who witnessed Lazarus walk out of the tomb hated Christ's influence so much that they would plot to kill Lazarus, the beneficiary of His power (John 12:9–11). He lamented that they recognized His genuine miracle but refused to receive Him as Lord. He mourned the Jews' rejection of Him that would quickly climax in a declaration with horrific implications:

> So when Pilate saw that he was getting nowhere, but rather that a riot was about to break out, he took water and washed his hands in the presence of the crowd, saying, "I am not guilty of nor responsible for this

righteous Man's blood; see to it yourselves." And all the people answered, "Let His blood be on us and on our children!" (Matthew 27:24–25, AMP).

To blind one's own eyes to the glory of God displayed through the miracles of Jesus, culminating in the raising of Lazarus, is amazingly defiant in itself. To implicate your children in your guilt is indescribable! You could argue that being willing to do the time for your own crime has a certain amount of virtue, but what can be said for insisting that your children be punished? How do you find words for people who set up their own children to take the fall for a murder rap? What else can be done for someone who hates you in proportion to the amount of love you show them? Jesus wept, anticipating the implications of their rejection more than the rejection itself.

The reasons for the people's rejection of Christ were as numerous as the voices that shouted, "Crucify Him!" They were jealous of Christ's influence. They coveted His power but despised His integrity. Many were disgusted over His humility in mingling with the poor and touching the untouchable. Others sought revenge for the embarrassment suffered when He exposed their sins and hypocrisy. Some saw Him as a threat to the social order and the political ties they had formed with corrupt Roman leaders. Others faulted Him for not being radical enough and leading an armed rebellion to overthrow the present order. Whatever their reasons were, they were effectively arguing for their release from His protective custody. " 'Jerusalem, Jerusalem, that kills the prophets, and stones those who are sent to her! How often I wanted to gather your children together, like a hen gathers her own brood under her wings, and you refused!' " (Luke 13:34, WEB).

What about us today? Are we defenders of the church's status quo even though we haven't been relevant in the surrounding community for decades? Has our dependence upon Christ been compromised by political activism? Is a sense of security in this world decreasing our desire for the Second Advent? Do we commend ourselves by saying, "At least I'm not like . . . "? Do we rate godliness according to material wealth? Do we avoid the evidence of answered prayers because we despise the self-denial required of Christians? Are we finding it easier to say no to invitations to the gospel? Is our conscience getting more comfortable with every repetition of the sin that used to make us shiver? Is it possible that Jesus is weeping not with us but for us?

> In every age there is given to men their day of light and privilege, a probationary time in which they may become reconciled to God. But there is a limit to this grace. Mercy may plead for years and be slighted and rejected; but there comes a time when mercy makes her last plea. The heart becomes so hardened that it ceases to respond to the Spirit of God (*The Desire of Ages*, 587).

> Christ saw in Jerusalem a symbol of the world hardened in unbelief and rebellion, and hastening on to meet the retributive judgments of God. The woes of a fallen race, pressing upon His soul, forced from His lips that exceeding bitter cry. He saw the record of sin traced in human misery, tears, and blood; His heart was moved with infinite pity for the afflicted and suffering ones of earth. . . . He was willing to pour out His soul unto death, to bring salvation within their reach; but few would come to Him that they might have life (*The Great Controversy*, 22).

Weeping *with* us was part of the desire that led our High Priest to dwell with us. Weeping *for* us grieves the Judge who seeks to pardon, not punish. Jesus wept then, and He weeps now. Is He weeping *with* you as your High Priest? Or weeping *for* you as your Judge?

5

Comforters, Inc.

Have you noticed that the longer you live, the more your definitions of young and old change? Remember when you thought thirty was old, and everything was downhill after that? What happened when you noticed thirty in your rearview mirror? Did you suddenly yearn to return to your youthful thirties? Have you also noticed that no matter how long your loved ones live, it's never long enough? Death alters our concept of age too, doesn't it?

Although death always occurs too soon, for older people we're able to put on a good face to celebrate a long, well-lived life. Promoting a positive spin when death's victim has barely begun to live requires more grit. In one church I pastored, we barely caught our breath from dealing with one premature loss when we got the wind knocked out of our souls by another. First a teenager, then an infant, and when it seemed it couldn't get any worse, a baby died a few short weeks before being born. Can you imagine being a mother whose womb becomes a tomb?

During those sorrowful times it feels as though we're called to weep with those who weep much more than to rejoice with those who rejoice (Romans 12:15). Paul Laurence Dunbar wrote about this skewed ratio of misery and mirth in his poem, "Life."

> *A crust of bread and a corner to sleep in,*
> *A minute to smile and an hour to weep in,*
> *A pint of joy to a peck of trouble,*
> *And never a laugh but the moans come double;*
> *And that is life!*

Is it any wonder that people are ensnared by addictions while seeking to soothe their sorrows? Southern Comfort™ is a natural choice for one who has not tasted supernatural comfort. Satan has a host of counterfeit comforters to medicate people if they're not acquainted with the Comforter.

Wait a minute . . . did I say *the* Comforter? Did you know Jesus not only speaks of *the* Comforter but also describes the Holy Spirit as *another* Comforter (John 14:16)? The word *another* implies there are at least two Comforters, but could there be more? How many Comforters are there? Is it possible that the Lord of Hosts has a host of comforters, an entourage of encouragers? It is worth investigating in this world where "the moans come double."

The first Comforter

Have you ever tried to reason with a friend who was about to do something incredibly stupid and who says, "I don't see anything wrong with that"? Weren't you tempted to smack him a couple of times and say, "What? Even Stevie Wonder can see what's wrong with that!" In many cases, these arguments aren't about right and wrong, just your opinion versus theirs. The stakes are low, and letting them make themselves look like a clown might be the best way to prove your point.

At other times, absolutes are involved, and the stakes are high. Whether it's a violation of physical, civil, or moral law, your friend's blindness to their course of action will have critical consequences. If you've warned your friend and shown alternate ways of doing things and they're still dancing with danger, there's a simple explanation: "A person who isn't spiritual doesn't accept the teachings of God's Spirit. He thinks they're nonsense. He can't understand them because a person must be spiritual to evaluate them" (1 Corinthians 2:14, GW). This lack of perception isn't accidental, for "the god of this world has blinded the minds of those who don't believe" (2 Corinthians 4:4, GW).

The enemy especially loves to blind our eyes when they're moist from mourning. If grief has you groping in confusion while this world's unrelenting pace presses you to make life-altering decisions in a moment's notice, then stop, drop, and pray. If you think you don't have time to pray, that's the enemy tightening the knot in the blindfold. You need the clarifying power of the Holy Spirit to avoid hasty decisions that promise quick relief, for they're usually yoked with burdens that cause even greater grief.

Yes, there's grace to cover every disgrace. Yes, we can learn from our mistakes. "Hindsight is 20/20," but do you want trial and error to be your travel guide? Not only will it be too late when you see what you did wrong but also you're likely to crash again because you're looking backward while speeding forward. So when you're craving comfort, when your self-medication isn't providing the peace you're seeking, when the side effects are causing more pain than the cure relieves, then it is time to "pray that the eyes of your heart may be enlightened, so that you will know what is the hope of His calling" (Ephesians 1:18, NASB). To borrow from Oliver Wendell Holmes, God will bless us with a "moment's insight" that "is sometimes worth a life's experience."

Why doesn't everyone seek the Spirit's wisdom, operate in His power, and enjoy His comfort? Didn't Jesus say the Father is more willing to give the Holy Spirit to those who ask than earthly fathers are willing to give gifts to their children (Luke 11:11–13)? Are we overlooking an obstacle that's tripping us up and preventing us from collecting this promise? In Acts 2:38, Peter says you should repent and be baptized and you will receive the gift of the Holy Ghost. Acts 5:32 adds that God gives the Holy Spirit to those who obey Him. These two passages teach us that clarification of truth results in our conviction of sin, righteousness, and judgment (John 16:8). Our comfort depends on our response to clarification and conviction.

What is conviction? It's the affliction of your conscience that takes place when the Spirit dangles your sins before your nose like a dirty diaper. His comfort doesn't come until we've confessed to our sin's stench. We can't have delusional expectations of God allowing us to stay grimy while making us smell good. God refuses to spray spiritual perfume on our mess. He insists on removing the garbage from our lives.

Seeking the Spirit's consolation while resisting clarification of truth and conviction of sin is like saying, "Yes" while shaking our heads "No." We must respond to clarification with obedience and to conviction with repentance. If not, then we seek a counterfeit comforter, because it violates the Spirit's job description to appease our guilty conscience.

Tempted to think the Spirit doesn't understand your circumstances that led to your misdeeds? The Spirit was grieved in Genesis 6, when the boundaries of grace bulged until the flood broke loose. The Spirit surrendered to humanity's rebellion and quit striving to bring conviction of sin and hope of salvation. People rejected the only power able to restrain the potential for evil residing within us all. Having closed their minds to Him, they became intoxicated with their evil imaginations. Ephesians 5:18 says we should not be drunk with wine but be filled with the Holy Ghost. It's an either/or proposition. If you're not filled with one thing, you'll be filled with another. As the antediluvians' lungs filled with water, they realized that grieving the Spirit only brings more grief. However, when we fill ourselves with the Spirit, we experience fruit that never ferments and we have highs without hangovers (see Galatians 5:22–23).

The second Comforter

If we say we have no sin, we are lying to God and deceiving ourselves (1 John 1:8–10). King David testified in the Psalms about how this self-deceit can have concrete consequences, such as undiagnosed physical pain. He later discovered that confession is a key to comfort, both spiritual and physical:

> When I refused to confess my sin, my whole body wasted away, while I groaned in pain all day long. For day and night you tormented me; you tried to destroy me in the intense heat of summer. . . . Then I confessed my sin; I no longer covered up my wrongdoing. I said, "I will confess my rebellious acts to the LORD. And then you forgave my sins (Psalm 32:3–5, *NET* Bible).

Some say, "You need to 'fess up when you mess up!" That's when our Advocate, Jesus Christ, can go to work for us. The word translated "advocate" in 1 John 2:1 is the same word (*paraclete*) translated Comforter in John's gospel. Why is the same Greek word translated into two

at English words? Ask yourself, why do we have so many words
for pants: slacks, jeans, trousers, khakis, overalls, britches? They all have
the basic purpose of covering our legs, but the different names indicate
the material they're made of, the setting they're worn in, or maybe even
your age (for those that wear britches). A *paraclete* is a helper who comes
alongside of one in need, to exhort, encourage, and even challenge.
Jesus and the Holy Spirit have similar yet distinct roles as *paracletes*, or
comforters. Both come alongside and intercede on our behalf.

> In the same way, the Spirit helps us in our weakness,
> for we do not know how we should pray, but the Spirit
> himself intercedes for us with inexpressible groanings.
> And he who searches our hearts knows the mind of
> the Spirit, because the Spirit intercedes on behalf of the
> saints according to God's will. . . . Who is the one who
> will condemn? Christ is the one who died (and more
> than that, he was raised), who is at the right hand of
> God, and who also is interceding for us (Romans 8:26,
> 27, 34, *NET* Bible).

The Holy Spirit and the Son work together like a laser in surgery
that cuts and cauterizes at the same time. We all have deeply embedded
malignant tumors called sins that God has to cut out in order for us to be
comforted. Our Great Physician won't put our souls at ease when we're
filled with sin's dis-ease. The Holy Spirit's incisions may pierce deeply,
but the simultaneous burning that occurs with conviction controls the
bleeding. Jesus won't let us die on the table. When we consent to Christ
taking every measure necessary, He'll remove our sins as far as the east
is from the west.

As we've seen already, Jesus understands our grief and then some.
His siblings didn't believe in Him (John 7:3–5). His treasurer betrayed
him, and His secretary of defense denied Him. He was alone in the
garden praying while the disciples slumbered. He wept over the city
that rejected Him, its true founder. He wept not for Himself but for the

disaster that would overtake them once they liberated themselves of His protective custody.

Yet we had better not presume that His understanding of our suffering leads Him to excuse our sin. His death proves the gravity of sin and is the most powerful argument for why we should repent—admit our guilt, ask forgiveness, and live to glorify Him. Paul writes that just as His death was sacrificial, our new life is sacrificial: "For the love of Christ controls us, since we have concluded this, that . . . He died for all so that those who live should no longer live for themselves but for him who died for them and was raised" (2 Corinthians 5:14–15, NET Bible). "Therefore I exhort you, brothers and sisters, by the mercies of God, to present your bodies as a sacrifice—alive, holy, and pleasing to God—which is your reasonable service" (Romans 12:1, NET Bible).

His high expectations of us might be depressing if He had not pledged to give us the desire and the power to perform the good works He has created us for (see Ephesians 2:10). "I am sure of this, that he who began a good work in you will bring it to completion at the day of Jesus Christ" (Philippians 1:6, ESV). "Therefore . . . work out your own salvation with fear and trembling, for it is God who works in you, both to will and to work for his good pleasure" (Philippians 2:12–13, ESV).

The third Comforter

Have you ever imagined God the Father as a cosmic cop with a righteous radar gun in one hand and a nightstick in the other? Does your mind's eye see Him hiding on the side of life's highway, waiting for an excuse to beat us down and lock us up? Did you know that a big part of why Jesus came is to clear up our caricatured ideas of the Father? Jesus didn't suffer in order to soften up a long-bearded grouch with a booming voice. His mission was to exemplify the power and love of the Father through His sacrificial life, death, and resurrection.

> In the beginning the Word already existed. The Word was with God, and the Word was God. . . . The Word became human and lived among us. We saw his glory.

It was the glory that the Father shares with his only Son, a glory full of kindness and truth. . . . No one has ever seen God. God's only Son, the one who is closest to the Father's heart, has made him known." " 'If you have known me, you will also know my Father. From now on you know him [through me] and have seen him in me' " (John 1:1, 14, 18; 14:7, GW).

The concept of God as a father figure is painfully difficult for some; they can't imagine it as a positive thing. However, this papa ain't no rolling stone. He's not seeking to get away from family obligations. He's seeking to enlarge His family circle through the Spirit's adoption, so He can extend His Son's enormous inheritance to all of us. It was the Father who so loved the world that He gave us His only begotten Son, so that whoever believes in Him will live eternally with Him in His house as a member of His family (see John 14:1–3; Romans 8:15; Hebrews 2:11; 1 John 3:1; Revelation 3:21).

In 2 Corinthians 1:3, we read that the Father is the God of all comfort. The God of *all* comfort means He's acquainted with the diversity of His children and what they're most susceptible to as individuals. He doesn't have just one way of dealing with His family members' distinct afflictions. I remember a hotel advertising that they have different kinds of pillows you can choose from. They know some people are comforted by soft, fluffy pillows while others prefer firm. Similarly, there are beds that adjust their levels of firmness and support with a remote control—a separate one for each side of the bed. People are different, even those pledged to be "one flesh" for the rest of their lives! Healthy relationships depend on us recognizing each other's uniqueness:

> Every association of life calls for the exercise of self-control, forbearance, and sympathy. We differ so widely in disposition, habits, education, that our ways of looking at things vary. We judge differently. Our

understanding of truth, our ideas in regard to the conduct of life, are not in all respects the same. There are no two whose experience is alike in every particular. The trials of one are not the trials of another. The duties that one finds light are to another most difficult and perplexing" (*Pathways to Health and Happiness*, 163).

Jesus showed His Father's recognition of our individuality through a wide variety of healing methods. For some He banished sickness with a verbal command. He imparted healing to others with a gentle touch, applying a mudpack, sticking His finger in their ears, or even spitting on their eyes! While some methods may seem strange and unpleasant, God designs unique, tailor-made comfort for each of us.

The Spirit identifying Himself as a Comforter presupposes the reality of affliction in the Christian life. The Father never deludes us with the false hope of "sweatless victory," as one TV preacher promised during a fundraising drive, but that there will be comfort during conflict. Controversy will persist until its perpetrators are consumed at the brightness of Christ's coming (2 Thessalonians 2:8). Jesus accomplished the Father's mission of saving us from the penalty from sin when He came the first time. He will rescue us from the presence of sin when He returns. Then we have the assurance, "Affliction shall not rise up a second time" (Nahum 1:9, KJV).

Instead of looking at God the Father through the negative experiences you may have had with your earthly father, or the void of having an absentee father, try looking at God as the father you wish you had. He's the Dad who is at your special events to make them more memorable. He's the Dad who's proud of your artwork when nobody can guess what it is. He's the Dad who makes strangers think twice about how they treat you. He's the Dad who forgives you and takes you back after you've wasted everything during your season of rebellion. He's the Dad who seems to know everything about everything but doesn't make you feel stupid that you don't. He's the Dad with a shoulder strong enough for everyone to cry on and is sympathetic enough not to mind our snot on His sleeve.

The Father Himself loves us and knows how much we need comfort. He not only sent His Son (John 3:16), but Jesus said it's the Father who sends the Spirit (John 14:26; Acts 1:4). Since the Father is responsible for sending Jesus and the Holy Spirit as comforters, He truly is the God of all comfort. Just open your favorite Bible app, look up "Father" in the New Testament, and experience His comfort for yourself.

The fourth Comforter

So the Bible reveals every member of the Godhead as a Comforter, and there's more? Who else would I dare list in this exclusive company of comforters? Actually, it's not who, but what. The Bible itself is the next Comforter!

It may seem like an ordinary book to our physical senses, but it comes alive when we open our hearts through prayer before we open its pages with our hands. Sometimes our other options must close before our hearts open. Sometimes His voice is most vivid when our situation is most hopeless. His Word will comfort us, if we'll pause to read it between crying and questioning. "Whatever things were written before were written for our learning, that we through patience and comfort of the Scriptures might have hope" (Romans 15:4, NKJV).

Notice the first part of the verse refers to what was "written before," as in the Old Testament—the Bible of Paul's day. The revelation of the God of all comfort didn't begin in the New Testament. God didn't start being gracious, merciful, and sympathetic in the book of Matthew. God had been setting the scene for Matthew, Mark, Luke, and John since Genesis 3:15!

I recently watched a TV personality evade difficult questions regarding the Old Testament by stating that Christians go by the New Testament instead of the Old. He further stated that the Old Testament stories couldn't be taken literally—they're basically fables. This was a ridiculous notion to the atheist he was debating, who was under the impression that Christians view the entire Bible as the Word of God. It's a sad commentary on the state of Christianity for me to agree with the atheist, rather than the Christian, on this point. That particular Christian doesn't realize that neglecting Old Testament study robs you of a source of comfort and a firm foundation for your New Testament study. As noted by Scott Ashley in his article, "The Old Testament in the New Testament":

> How many times do the writers of the New Testament *quote* the Old Testament? An index in the Jewish New Testament catalogs *695 separate quotations* from the books of the Old Testament in the New (Jewish New Testament Publications, Jerusalem, 1989). There are many other passages where the Old Testament is *referred to*, as in cases where an Old Testament figure is mentioned, but no specific scripture is quoted. Depending on which scholar's work you examine, the number of quotations and references in the New Testament to the Old may be as high as *4,105* (Roger Nicole, *The Expositor's Bible Commentary*, Zondervan, Grand Rapids, 1979, Vol. I, p. 617).[1]

In other words, we don't have much of a New Testament if we subtract the Old. Don't take my word for it, though, or the word of theologians and commentators. The words of Christ Himself let us know the importance of being acquainted with the Old Testament, for we cannot know Him without it:

> Then Jesus said to them, "How foolish you are! You're so slow to believe everything the prophets said! Didn't the Messiah have to suffer these things and enter into his glory?" Then he began with Moses' Teachings and the Prophets to explain to them what was said about him throughout the Scriptures. . . . They said to each

1. Scott Ashley, "The Old Testament in the New Testament," *Good News Magazine*, March–April 1998, http://www.ucg.org/christian-living/old-testament-new-testament/.

other, 'Weren't we excited when he talked with us on the road and opened up the meaning of the Scriptures for us?' " (Luke 24:25–27, 32, GW).

Few people in history have been more heartbroken than Jesus' disciples at the crucifixion. Yet Jesus didn't immediately dispel their despondency through miraculous means. He insisted on building their faith, verse by verse. A quick fix would have set them up for future hopelessness. It's difficult for me to explain any better than through this passage in *The Desire of Ages*:

> Had He first made Himself known to them, their hearts would have been satisfied. In the fullness of their joy they would have hungered for nothing more. But it was necessary for them to understand the witness borne to Him by the types and prophecies of the Old Testament. . . . They had looked upon His death as the destruction of all their hopes. Now He showed from the prophets that this was the very strongest evidence for their faith. . . . The miracles of Christ are a proof of His divinity; but a stronger proof that He is the world's Redeemer is found in comparing the prophecies of the Old Testament with the history of the New (796–799).

Since the Old Testament served as the basis for the Savior's consolation to His grief-stricken disciples, how can we ignore that large portion of the Bible and yet find comfort in Christ? Don't deprive yourself of solace by divorcing what the Savior has joined together.

The Scriptures acquaint us with the Comfort offered by the Father, Son, and Holy Spirit. Since the weeping that endures for a night feels as though morning will bring more mourning than joy, and since the ratio of time provides only "a minute to smile and an hour to weep in," it only makes sense for us to balance the emotional scales of life's trauma with every comforting verse we can find from one cover of the Bible to the other.

The fifth Comforter

"Wherefore comfort yourselves together, and edify one another" (1 Thessalonians 5:11). "A new commandment I give unto you, that ye love one another" (John 13:34). "Be kindly affectioned one to another" (Romans 12:10). "Have the same care one for another" (1 Corinthians 12:25). "By love serve one another" (Galatians 5:13). "Bear ye one another's burdens" (Galatians 6:2). "Confess your faults one to another, and pray one for another, that ye may be healed" (James 5:16). "Submitting yourselves one to another in the fear of God" (Ephesians 5:21). "Teaching and admonishing one another in psalms and hymns and spiritual songs" (Colossians 3:16). "But exhort one another daily" (Hebrews 3:13). "Have fellowship one with another" (1 John 1:7). "Use hospitality one to another without grudging" (1 Peter 4:9). "Be subject one to another" (1 Peter 5:5). "Be ye all of one mind, having compassion one of another" (1 Peter 3:8). "Be ye kind one to another, tenderhearted, forgiving one another" (Ephesians 4:32). "Wherefore comfort one another with these words" (1 Thessalonians 4:18).

That's just a sample of the "one another" commands the Bible uses to spur the fifth Comforter to live up to its calling. You may call her the bride of Christ, the body of Christ, or you might even have some derogatory terms for her—but the church is the fifth Comforter. I'm not talking about the building with the stained glass and steeple. I'm talking about the clergy and congregations that need reminders that church isn't a place of worship but the worshipers themselves. When our praise is life service (versus lip service), we become co-comforters with the Father, Son, Holy Spirit, and the Scriptures.

That doesn't denigrate God, but it elevates us. We're granted the privilege to perform hands-on application of the comfort we've received from Him. When we participate in His mission, we partake of His character. The Bible declares that the church is the body of Christ and we are individual members of the body. As the head, He expects of us the same things that we expect from our body parts—cooperation. Only diseased bodies have limbs that don't execute the wishes and commands of the mind. In many cases, life can be saved despite the loss of limbs. Sometimes the preservation of life demands amputation of diseased members. However, the survival rate for head amputees is very low! Jesus is the only indispensable part of this body.

We as individual members have value as we perform what the head transmits to us. How do we make sure our receptors function correctly? Through prayer, study, and repetition of His will. There is this thing called muscle memory in our physical bodies that has a spiritual counterpart. "That which at first seems difficult, by constant repetition grows easy, until right thoughts and actions become habitual" (*Character Construction*, 34). As we learn more about the comfort of the Father, Son, and Holy Spirit through the comfort of the Scriptures, opportunities will open for us to become incorporated with the rest of the comforters. Of course, we comfort one another with the objective knowledge of God as revealed in Scripture.

We also comfort others by relating our subjective experience of how God comforted us (2 Corinthians 1:4). Sharing our stories may make us feel uncomfortable and vulnerable, but temporary discomfort is the price we pay for the privilege of being co-comforters with Christ. You may be inconvenienced, and your feelings might get hurt. But you don't shy away from the call of being a comforter out of fear that you will be discomforted! Solomon said that the dead and the unborn are better off than the living, because he observed a lack of comforters in the world (see Ecclesiastes 4:1–3). Let's all do our part so that no one feels that they are better off dead.

Sometimes we question and blame God for not providing comfort to someone in need. The ironic thing is that He might very well be blaming us for the same things. The Father, Son, Holy Spirit, and Holy Scriptures invite and equip us to join Comforters, Inc. Won't you accept the privilege of promoting healing and populating heaven? Together we can help fulfill the closing thoughts of Dunbar's poem:

A crust and a corner that love makes precious,
With a smile to warm and the tears to refresh us;
And joy seems sweeter when cares come after,
And a moan is the finest of foils for laughter;
And that is life!

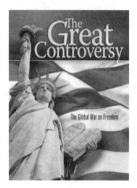
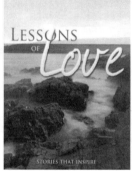

Carl McRoy (Pastor Mac) is an ordained minister and freelance writer. He can be reached at yagal1135@gmail.com

To add some of Pastor McRoy's favorites to your favorites, contact the Family Health Education Service at: 404-299-1621 and tell them Pastor Mac sent you.